A Choral Suite: *Soprano/Alto/Tenor/Bass and Piano*

Music by
Duke Ellington,
Billy Strayhorn,
Mercer Ellington,
Harry Lenk &
Ervin Drake

Lyrics by
Billy Strayhorn,
Johnny Mercer,
Ted Persons &
Juan Tizol

Arranged by
Hywel Davies

Suite comprises:
Take The 'A' Train
Satin Doll
Lush Life
Things Ain't What They Used To Be
Perdido

A DUKE ELLINGTON SUITE

Novello

A Duke Ellington Choral Suite

1 TAKE THE 'A' TRAIN

Words & Music by
Billy Strayhorn

4

attacca

2 SATIN DOLL

Words by Johnny Mercer
Music by Duke Ellington & Billy Strayhorn

1. Ci-ga-rette hol-der which wigs me o-ver her shoul-der, she digs me
2. Ba-by shall we go out skip-pin' care-ful a-mi-go, you're flip-pin'

for rehearsal only

attacca

3 LUSH LIFE

Words and Music by
Billy Strayhorn

12

Lyrics:
washed a - way by too ma-ny through the day twelve o' clock tales (Soprano)
washed a - way by too ma-ny through the day twelve o' clock tales Then (Alto)
you came a - long with your si - ren song to tempt me to mad - ness. (Tenor)
I thought for a while that your poig - nant smile was ting'd with a sad - ness

attacca

4 THINGS AIN'T WHAT THEY USED TO BE

Words by Ted Persons
Music by Mercer Ellington

attacca

5 PERDIDO

Words by Juan Tizol
Music by Harry Lenk and Ervin Drake

*The ♪ indicates a shorter, more rhythmic 'snap' than the swung quaver ♪♪

published by Novello Publishing Limited
Music setting by Stave Origination
Printed in Great Britain

Novello Voices

Novello Voices is a new series, designed to bring you great songs, newly arranged in contemporary choral style.
The series includes:

Choral Suites

Superbly arranged Soprano/Alto/Tenor/Bass concert suites containing selections of best-known songs and numbers from hit musicals:

The Phantom of the Opera
Les Misérables
Aspects of Love
Miss Saigon
Evita
Joseph and the Amazing Technicolor Dreamcoat
Yesterday Once More (The Carpenters)
Good Vibrations (The Beach Boys)
A Duke Ellington Suite
Showboat
Revolver (The Beatles)

Show Singles

West End and Braodway show-stoppers, newly arranged for Soprano/Alto/Tenor/Bass and Piano:

DON'T CRY FOR ME, ARGENTINA (from *Evita*)
ON THIS NIGHT OF A THOUSAND STARS (from *Evita*)
CLOSE EVERY DOOR (from *Joseph*)
ANY DREAM WILL DO (from *Joseph*)
LOVE CHANGES EVERYTHING (from *Aspects of Love*)
SEEING IS BELIEVING (from *Aspects of Love*)
ALL I ASK OF YOU (from *The Phantom of the Opera*)
WISHING YOU WERE SOMEHOW HERE AGAIN
  (from *The Phantom of the Opera*)
BRING HIM HOME (from *Les Misérables*)
CASTLE ON A CLOUD (from *Les Misérables*)
THE LAST NIGHT OF THE WORLD (from *Miss Saigon*)
THE AMERICAN DREAM (from *Miss Saigon*)

Order No. NOV160261

ISBN 978-0-85360-590-4

Novello Voices

Novello Publishing Limited
14-15 Berners Street, London W1T 3LJ.

Exclusive distributors:
Hal Leonard Europe Limited
Distribution Centre, Newmarket Road
Bury St Edmunds Suffolk, IP33 3YB
www.halleonard.com

DISTRIBUTED BY HAL LEONARD

8 84088 48571 9

14009357

EXCLUSIVELY DISTRIBUTED BY
HAL•LEONARD